corvette

AMERICAN ✳ ICONS

corvette

LARRY STEVENS

An imprint of Globe Pequot

Distributed by NATIONAL BOOK NETWORK

British Library Cataloguing in Publication Information available

Library of Congress Cataloging-in-Publication Data available

ISBN 978-1-4930-3298-3 (hardcover)
ISBN 978-1-4930-3299-0 (e-book)

Cover and interior design by Vertigo Design NYC

♾™ The paper used in this publication meets the minimum requirements of American National Standard for Information Sciences—Permanence of Paper for Printed Library Materials, ANSI/NISO Z39.48-1992.

Printed in the United States of America

CONTENTS

THE CORVETTE STORY

Executives at General Motors were inspired to create a homegrown sports car after American GIs from WWII began shipping home "souvenirs" from Europe like Jaguars, MGs, and Alfa Romeos.

The idea of the Corvette was to be the American version of European sports cars. The Corvette was built to compete with its European rivals at a more affordable price point.

Safety wasn't first . . . at first

FOR THE FIRST FIVE MODEL YEARS, the Chevrolet Corvette did not offer a restraint system. Seat belts weren't factory installed until the 1958 model.

THE FIRST CORVETTE WAS INTRODUCED IN 1953 and was offered with one color option: a white convertible with red interior.

The original crossed-flags Corvette emblem featured a checkered flag on the right and the U.S. flag on the left. Four days before the car made its debut at the 1953 Motorama, it was redesigned to avoid the frowned-upon "use of Old Glory for advertising purposes."

Harley Earl, the GM designer considered the "father" of the Corvette, couldn't fit inside his creation. At 6´3˝ tall, his head hovered far above the curved windshield. Earl knew the car had to be stylish in order to grab the attention of potential buyers.

FAST FACTS

- Only 300 Corvettes were released that first year back in 1953.

- 1,595,026 Corvettes have been manufactured from 1953–2017.

- Corvette is the official car of the state of Kentucky.

- The first Corvette to roll out was a convertible. Every Corvette currently offered has a convertible option.

- The 2017 Z06 coupe and convertible have 650 HP of pure power under the hood.

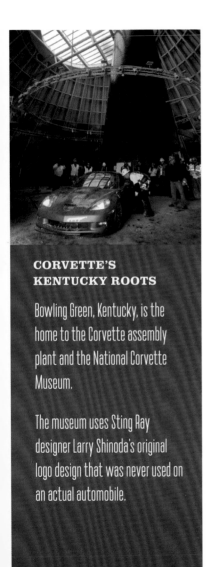

UNDER THE HOOD

The V8 engine in a Corvette has eight cylinders laid out in a V-formation. It's the power behind the engine's roar. Although Corvettes typically cost a lot less than their European counterparts, they pack just as much power under the hood.

GENERAL MOTORS & CHEVROLET

Chevrolet was founded in 1911 (the same year the Indianapolis 500 began!) to compete with the Model T Ford. In 1915, the company released its first true competitor to the Model T—the Model 490 was $5 less at a total price tag of $490.

Chevrolet joined GM a few years later in 1918. As a division of GM, Chevy turned Corvette dreams into reality, and in 1953 the first Corvette showed up on the scene.

WHAT'S IN THE NAME?

MYRON E. SCOTT is the man to take credit for naming the Corvette, but what is the origin? Scott, a newspaper photographer, submitted the name along with hundreds of other names and was the winner. The name is from a fast-strike ship from WWII, and Scott felt that not only is it a great sounding name for a car, but would appeal to American men who fought during the war.

Scott started his career as an artist, photographer, and art director at the *Dayton Daily News*. It was in 1933 that he photographed six boys racing wooden boxes and it's where he got the idea for a "soap box derby." The Derby initially brought in 330 participants and drew a crowd of 40,000 to watch. Chevrolet actually decided to sponsor the event and continued sponsoring until 1972.

Chevrolet hired Scott in 1937 as an assistant director for Public Relations, but it was 1953 that would put him in Corvette folklore. When looking for a name to their new sports vehicle, Chevrolet wanted the name to start with the letter *c*. They received over 300 submissions and none of them really appealed to the executive team at Chevrolet. That is, not until Scott, looked through the *c* section of the dictionary to find Corvette, which was described as "a pursuit ship in the British navy."

DID YOU KNOW?

The name Corvette didn't originate with these WWII ships. It goes way back to 1670s France. The French Navy ships known as corvettes were smaller and highly maneuverable, giving them a huge advantage over the larger ships.

Corvette ships are still used today!

THE GODFATHER OF THE CORVETTE

ZORA ARKUS-DUNTOV was the man who transformed the car into the sports car it is today.

Born in Belgium, he grew up studying engineering and driving race cars.

He moved to the U.S. and started his career at GM in 1953 as an assistant engineer.

Although he loved the look of the Corvette when he first started at GM, he didn't like what was under the hood and made some suggestions, going as far as writing a letter to the head engineer, suggesting that the car should have a V8 engine.

In 1957, Zora was promoted to the head of high-performance vehicles at GM, and by 1968 became chief engineer of the Corvette, a dream job for him.

In 1975, Zora finally retired, leaving behind a legacy of tremendous achievements. He remained a tremendous promoter of the vehicle he helped create, even showing up to the celebration of the 1 millionth Corvette at the Bowling Green Assembly plant.

He passed away in 1996, but his legacy lives on, and an upcoming Corvette is rumored to be named after him.

"To establish the sports car, you have to race it."
—ZORA ARKUS-DUNTOV

THE LARRY SHINODA & BILL MITCHELL COLLABORATION

LARRY SHINODA was known for a number of innovative car designs, most notably the Stingray.

Shinoda was born on March 25, 1930, in Los Angeles, California. During World War II, the U.S. government forced him and his family into an internment camp for those of Japanese heritage. He built hot rods as a young adult and drag raced them across Los Angeles. In 1955 (at the age of twenty-five), he won the first ever National Hot Rod Associaion (NHRA) finals in Great Bend, Kansas.

He started his career at General Motors competitor, Ford Motor Company, but stayed there for just one year. In 1956, he was working with the GM styling team where he eventually met Bill Mitchell. It was at the infamous "Studio X" that Shinoda helped to create Mitchell's concept of the Stingray.

It took the "Shinoda touch" to help Mitchell's design come to life and ultimately result in the beautiful automotive machine powered by Arkus-Duntov's engineering team.

THE ICONIC CAR has had many great years, but they weren't all rousing successes . . . Take the first model released in 1953: It was nicknamed "the rolling bathtub" due to its initial appearance and performance. From its humble beginnings, the Corvette took shape and quickly became the top name in iconic American sports car history.

> *"You got to realize that when I was 20 years old, I had a house, a Mercedes, a Corvette, and a million dollars in the bank before I could buy alcohol legally."* —DR. DRE

Less Truth in Advertising

1954 was another lackluster year for the car. Not because of its design or performance, but because of its price point. The car was advertised at a base sticker price of $2,774.00—before the "luxury" add-ons like a two-speed Powerglide transmission, windshield wipers, and a heater, which drove the price above $3,000. A steep price for any car those days. Consumers voted with their wallets that year—almost half of the units produced remained unsold at the end of the production year.

HOLD THE CLUTCH

In 1982, the Bowling Green plant rolled out its first model, but the company seemed so intent on operations, they paid little attention to the overall design, taking bits and pieces from previous models and packing them into the 1982 offering. This model marked the first to offer only automatic transmission, leaving manual enthusiasts out of luck.

1982 also marked the end of the C3 era, however, so a special Collectors Edition was released, but the price point was high and consumers once again voted with their checkbook. It was the first Corvette to break the $22,000 price point.

When Power Wasn't a Means or an End

Another failure, the 1984 fourth-generation model was seen as uncomfortable, difficult to maintain, clunky, and overall unreliable.

The C3 had a long run, from 1968 to 1982. Some of the models in that time didn't quite make the grade, like the 1979 model. which looked very much like the 1978 model. Without the special Indy 500 Pace Car and Silver Anniversary Edition enhancements, there was little to make it stand out. The 1979 C3 was a great seller, but not a standout model for collectors or even drivers at the time.

"It's a matter of always raising expectations by never standing still."

— TADGE JUECHTER, CORVETTE

17

Farewell to Zora

Zora Arkus-Duntov retired on January 1, 1975, leaving many enthusiasts wondering what would become of the brand he saved and nurtured for decades. For this reason, confidence was already low when new emissions standards were released, eliminating lead-based gas and introducing catalytic converters. These changes took the engine's power from 270 down to 165. The new engine was a disappointment, but the car still sold well. A testament to the life's work and passion of Mr. Arkus-Duntov.

CORVETTE'S TOP MODELS

The Vette has had many top hits, but each model has one claim to fame that rose above the rest.

The Solid Axle
('53-'62)

The Sting Ray
('63-'67)

The Mako Shark
('68-'82)

Scientific Corvettes
('84-'96)

World Beater
('97-'04)

Power Player
('05-'13)

Starship Stingray
('14-Present)

Little did anyone know during the 50s that a true iconic legend was created.

C1 THE ORIGINAL (1953-1962)

This is the decade the Corvette was born—1953 to be exact. Consumers didn't have many choices with this model year, with one option—white exterior and red interiors.

Who's the man behind the name? Myron Scott, a newspaper photographer, is credited with naming the Corvette, after the WWII strike ships.

Rivals burst onto the scene, with cars such as the Ford Thunderbird also including a V8 engine and other sports car luxuries.

Corvette kept forging ahead, and never lost ground in this decade, leaving competitors in the dust.

The only options available on the original 1953 Corvette were an interior heater and an AM radio. There was no hard top, and there were no roll-up windows.

It was the year 1954 that introduced Corvette to its new Chief Engineer, Zora Arkus-Duntov, who would take the vehicle to the next level, including changing its engine's horsepower.

The 51st Corvette ever built was owned by the legend himself, John Wayne. At 6´4˝, Wayne couldn't have found the tiny car a very comfortable fit, and his future cars were all giant wagons. One even featured a customized raised roof so he could wear his cowboy hat while he drove!

Another red-hot C1 was driven by Johnny Depp when he portrayed Paul Kemp in Hunter S. Thompson's flick The Rum Diaries. In this drug and alcohol-fueled romp, the car is featured heavily throughout the story and lives on in Depp's private collection. The car was gifted to him by one of the film's producers after shooting wrapped.

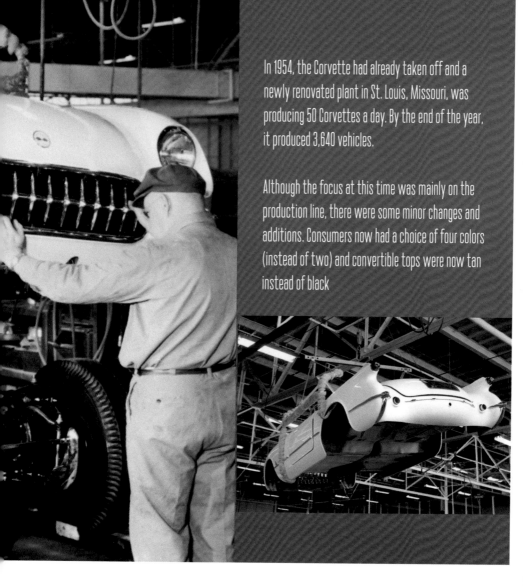

In 1954, the Corvette had already taken off and a newly renovated plant in St. Louis, Missouri, was producing 50 Corvettes a day. By the end of the year, it produced 3,640 vehicles.

Although the focus at this time was mainly on the production line, there were some minor changes and additions. Consumers now had a choice of four colors (instead of two) and convertible tops were now tan instead of black

David Lee Roth's song "Sensible Shoes" is a song about feeling empty despite having it all, including a good job and a Corvette Stingray.

C2 THE STING RAY (1963-1967)

The sixties had a lot of monumental moments (rocket ship to the moon!), but in Vette history, there's nothing more iconic than the Sting Ray, which is the most famous of all Corvette names.

With the Sting Ray, the Corvette saw a fairly dramatic over-haul, which improved road handling and upped the level of performance. The reviews were stellar, suggesting that the Corvette was now second to none for road handling while maintaining the impressive power.

The Sting Ray was first introduced as a concept design that was folded into the second gener-ation of the Vette.

The first design
when this model was
introduced had a split
rear window, which
created some in-fighting
with the design team.
The "godfather" of the
Vette, lead engineer
Zora Arkus-Duntov
suggested that it
impeded the driver's
view. Duntov ultimately
won and the next
iterations—starting
with the '64 model—
didn't include the split
window.

The Big-Block engine was added to the Corvette in the 1965 model (6.5 liter, L78 and over 400 horse-power), which required a new hood to fit this massive power plant.

The power kept expanding well into the late 60s when Corvette horsepower peaked at more than 500.

The 1963 Corvette was built under the direction of GM's Head of Design, Bill Mitchell, who based the car's exterior on a mako shark he caught during a recent deep-sea fishing trip.

STEALING THE SPOTLIGHT FROM ELVIS HIMSELF

By the late 1960s, Elvis Presley was tired of making campy movies, but he still went along for the ride. While the 1967 flick *Clambake* was a lackluster bust with unmemorable songs, Elvis's 1959 one-of-a-kind Sting Ray Racer stole the show, winning the 1960 SCCA C-Modified Championship. For the movie, the car was painted candy-apple red and fitted with a Big-Block engine and clear plexi, snorkel-type scoop.

TO THE MOON!

These days, the Corvette is as iconically American as apple pie and Route 66, but the car had a slow start. Up until its introduction, cars had been big and solid. The little fiberglass convertible looked more like a toy than an actual automobile. But Chevrolet, the makers of the little engines that could, plugged ahead with brilliant celebrity endorsements, pairing the car with other iconically American giants like John Wayne.

In 1961, astronaut Alan Shepherd received a surprising gift shortly after becoming the first American to travel into outer space: a 1962 Corvette. Shepherd loved his first Vette so much, he owned ten throughout his lifetime.

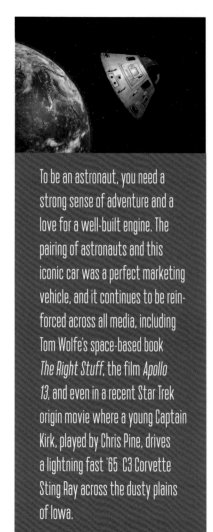

To be an astronaut, you need a strong sense of adventure and a love for a well-built engine. The pairing of astronauts and this iconic car was a perfect marketing vehicle, and it continues to be reinforced across all media, including Tom Wolfe's space-based book *The Right Stuff*, the film *Apollo 13*, and even in a recent Star Trek origin movie where a young Captain Kirk, played by Chris Pine, drives a lightning fast '65 C3 Corvette Sting Ray across the dusty plains of Iowa.

THE RIGHT STUFF

The 1960s marked the age of the astronaut.
Every kid wanted to be one, and every adult was fascinated by their mettle and the excitement of space travel. Jim Rathmann, the winner of the Indianapolis 500 in 1960, left racing to settle down and become a Chevrolet dealer in Florida. He saw the cachet of space travel and proposed a campaign that changed the face of Corvette history. He arranged with the company to lease Corvettes to the spacemen for only a dollar apiece. Six of the seven astronauts took the company up on their offer, and often posed for pics with their new cars, despite NASA's fears that it would look like an official endorsement. (John Glenn opted for a Chevy wagon instead.) Despite NASA's concerns, photos of the Apollo 12 astronauts and their matching, custom cars appeared in *Life* magazine in 1971, and the Apollo 15 crew posed alongside their red, white, and blue Vettes and a Lunar Rover.

Tom Hanks was so taken by his experience starring in Apollo 13 ***that he was inspired to create the 1998 HBO miniseries*** From the Earth to the Moon. ***His portrayal kept a close eye on accuracy, which of course meant featuring several astronaut-owned Corvettes in the series.***

C3 THE STINGRAY (1968-1982)

In 1968, we were introduced to the third generation of the Corvette, which was based on the Mako Shark II car showcased in 1965 as a concept car.

The C3 had the longest run of any of their generations, spanning over fifteen years.

The change from the Sting Ray to the Stingray did more than condensing the name to one word; it created a whole new look that was to become the new standard for Corvette over a number of years.

The rolling hood that was a part of this new design
is still a part of the Corvette today.

1979

Due to the changing times, *the C3 tried to adapt,* converting to a less-powerful engine to meet the increased emission standards.

Even though power was decreased, the C3 set an *all-time sales record* in 1979 of 58,307 that year—that record still stands today.

The 250,000th Corvette to roll off the production line was a 1969 Stingray. It was a gold convertible emblazoned with the word "Stingray" above the fender.

"Let's face it, the Corvette is three feet too long and 800 pounds too heavy . . . the seats are awful and the rear suspension does weird things. But within the next two years, you're going to see a serious effort to make the car better."

— A GM ENGINEER, 1976

The design of the frame shouts power and it's not lying. The insides were equally as impressive, with a 400-horsepower 427 cu. in. engine.

C4 (1984-1996)

Although the C4 series was defined as an 80s Vette, it didn't come out until 1984, due to a ton of delays, and production ran through the mid-90s.

The inside of the car was equally as impressive, introducing the first digital display. Moving from analog to digital was a huge step for the Corvette, but a necessary one to keep up with consumers' cravings for cutting-edge tech and engineering.

Changes were made immediately after the first C4, creating more horsepower by the next year's model (1985).

In 1986, the convertible was back, along with anti-lock brakes and a little extra horsepower.

The vehicle won *Motor Trend's* Car of the Year award when it was released in '84.

MOTORTREND CAR OF THE YEAR ®

WWE WRESTLING RIVALRY CEMENTED IN HISTORY: *Car enthusiasts everywhere cringed when "Stone Cold" Steve Austin backed up a cement truck into the wrestling arena and filled rival Vince McMahon's beautiful C4 with cement in a very impractical joke. There's even a clip of the whole thing online if you can bear to watch.*

It was in '86 that Corvette was back at the Indy 500. It was none other than Chuck Yeager, the first person to break the sound barrier, who drove the pace car.

The 1,000,0000th Corvette came off the assembly line on July 2, 1992, where some of the most notable engineers and designers were on hand to witness this incredible milestone, including none other than Zora Arkus-Duntov, the "godfather" of the Corvette.

The ZR1 model produced during the C4 series period had a horsepower that was available from '90 to '95 and its horsepower rose to 405 by '93, which coincidentally was Corvette's 40th anniversary.

C5 (1997-2004)

After four years of delays, the fifth generation finally debuted in '97. Its much-awaited arrival pleased even the toughest critics. Built from the ground up, the C5 amped up the horsepower while streamlining aerodynamic design, all while keeping comfort and appearance top of mind. This user-friendly model was as easy on the eyes as it was on the road. It could accelerate from 0–60 in less than 4 seconds, while its widened wheel base, larger rear tires, and cutting-edge suspension made for an easy, comfortable driving experience.

In 1998, Chevrolet released the C5 convertible. The '98 version ran slightly lighter than its predecessors, thanks to run-flat tires that eliminated the need for a spare and a semi-automatic convertible top without the bulky mechanics. Since both the spare and the roof mechanics normally take up significant back-end real-estate, the C5 has a fair amount of trunk space—something a Corvette hadn't featured since '62.

Corvette brought back road racing in '98 with their race cars, the C5-Rs created some serious waves on the circuit, winning the GTS class at Le Mans and the American Le Mans Series Manufacturers' Championship in 2001. The C5-R won the American Le Mans Series Manufacturer's Championship again in '02 and '03.

In 2003, Corvette celebrated its 50th anniversary. In honor of this milestone, Chevy created an ANNIVERSARY EDITION, which included a special color scheme: RED PAINT, CHAMPAGNE COLORED WHEELS, AND GRAY-BEIGE LEATHER UPHOLSTERY.

One could get this edition in both the coupe and convertible models but not the Z06.

Best in Show

Motor Trend magazine named the 2003 Z06 the best Corvette to date. *Motor Trend* gave it top overall honors that year, stating that the car's sexy look, high performance, fuel efficiency and all-around American attitude put it above its European competitors.

In 2004, to commemorate the racing achievements, Corvette came out with an option to order any of the three models available in a special Le Mans Blue.

C6 (2005-2013)

The 2005 model of the C6 introduced coupe and convertible versions. This was the first year that Corvette introduced both a hard top and roofless version in the same year!

The design of the C6 was a major focus, producing a shorter and narrower car.

The C6 was created and developed by chief engineer David Hill and designer Tom Peters.

The performance and overall style of the C6 series was highly praised by both experts and buyers.

The ZR1 was the first Corvette to hit 200 mph.

"LIFE BEGINS AT 200 MPH"

—MOTTO ON THE OFFICIAL ZR1 T-SHIRT

The ZO6 version of the C6 came onto the scene in 2006 with a whopping **505** horsepower engine.

In 2012, General Motors celebrated its 100th year. Corvette was, of course, part of the centennial celebration, with a special package offered that included a Carbon Flash metallic paint, special interior, and even centennial badges, along with a ton of other features.

It was during the C6 era that the economy went through the "Great Recession" and overall vehicle sales took a hit. The Corvette, however, reintroduced the Grand Sport name in 2010, which equated to almost half of their overall sales that year.

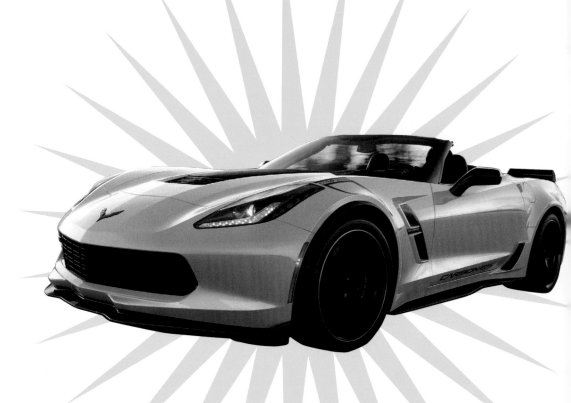

2018: *In celebration of Corvette's 65th year, the Carbon 65 is available on both the Grand Sport 3LT and Z06 3LZ models. It is produced in only one color—ceramic matrix gray in a limited run of 650 (450 in the U.S. and 200 as exports).*

C7 (2014-PRESENT)

The 2014 Corvette Stingray made its introduction and strutted its stuff at the Detroit Auto Show in 2013.

It was packed with power—coming in with a 455 HP, 6.2 liter pushrod, V8 engine.

Although celebrities like the classic Corvettes, there are a number of stars and TV characters who drive some C7s, including Paul Stanley from KISS and his 2015 Stingray, Paris Hilton's very pink C7, and *Marvel's Agents of S.H.I.E.L.D.* Agent Coulson's hot red 1962 Sting Ray that he nicknamed Lola.

CORVETTES BY THE NUMBERS

ALL-TIME BEST SELLER

The winning year for Corvette was **1979,** with **53,807** C3s sold that year. The record low sales year goes to, yep, 1953—the first year out of the gate, with a whopping 300 units sold. Little did they know that this would lead to one of the most famous American icons ever.

STARTING PRICE

The first Corvettes were advertised at a base price under **$2,775,** which included an AM radio and heater. But adding the two-speed Powerglide transmission and windshield wipers pushed the cost nearer **$3,500.**

The best way to judge speed in a sports vehicle is how fast it can get from 0–60, and we tracked this performance throughout the years.

- **1953** was off to a slow start, given that it would be two years before the introduction of the V8 engine. Even with a smaller engine, this great-looking vehicle could get from 0–60 in **11 seconds**.

- In **1955,** with the V8 engine, the Vette got from 0–60 in over 2 seconds less time, clocking in at **8.7 seconds**.

- WOW! In **1967,** the engine was equipped with a 435 HP, L98 engine, which got the 0–60 metric down to **4.7 seconds**.

- The C3 was subject to emissions regulations and in **1978,** the 0–60's slowest time yet was clocked at **7.8 seconds**.

- Then things got back on track again in **1990,** reaching 60 MPH in **4.5 seconds** with the ZR1 model, which finally outdid the 1967 L98 engine

- **2002** really stepped up its game, getting an engine to hit 60 MPH in **under 4 seconds** (3.4 seconds to be exact), with the Z06 model and then matched again with the ZR1.

- **In recent years,** with the introduction of the C7, the Vette finally hit the **3-second mark**.

No one knows if the times can get even shorter, but rest assured the General Motors team is working on it.

13 SPECIAL CORVETTES IN MARKET

ACCORDING TO *ROAD AND TRACK* MAGAZINE

The Corvette is already known as one of the fastest machines, but here are some Vettes that are considered among the fastest . . .

Corvette Z06 The first Z06 built in '62 for the '63 model year had, and needed, a great cooling system to keep everything running smoothly.

Corvette L88 This machine was built for the racetrack and only 216 were made. It is one of the most sought-after Corvettes ever made.

Corvette Grand Sport Only five of these puppies were built, but man do they look super cool. So cool, they can go for between $6–$8 million.

Corvette ZR1 A bit smaller than the L88 at 370 HP (compared to 435), it came with tons of style and flare to put it on the list.

Corvette Sting Ray 427 This lighter-weight model with incredible engine and horsepower made this one fast machine.

Corvette ZR1 At 375 HP, it puts it only 5 HP away from the famous Ferrari Testarossa and came from the collaboration of the Mercury Marine and Lotus.

Corvette Grand Sport The last C4 model, this one with an extra 30 HP over regular Corvettes. It came in only one color—"Admiral Blue Metallic"

Corvette Grand Sport This was a way to get all the Z06 parts at a lower cost, and oh, by the way, still looks incredibly cool.

Corvette Z06 The engine bumped up to 405 HP, which needed a different clutch and gearing system to better handle all this additional power.

Corvette 427 Convertible Power and a convertible! This 505 HP V8 and the top comes down! It was made to celebrate Corvette's 60th anniversary.

Corvette Z06 The third VO6 on the market and Chevy went all in on the HP, increasing it to 505. Check this out— 0–60 in 3.8 seconds.

Corvette Z06 The first supercharged Z06, it's 650 HP. For under $80K, you can get one of the fastest cars on the market, although it's had overheating issues on the track.

Corvette ZR1 When released, it was considered the most powerful GM car ever produced, coming in at a whopping 638 HP.

"We kicked Ferrari's rear at less than half the price. What's not to like?"

— CORVETTE ENGINEER, 2008

10 MOST VALUABLE CORVETTES

ACCORDING TO CNN MONEY

1 '63 GRAND SPORT

$6–$8 million due to a limited production run of only five.

2 '69 CORVETTE ZL1

$1.4 million with a limited production of two of its kind.

3 '67 CORVETTE L88 CONVERTIBLE

$1 million with a limited run of just 20.

4 '69 CORVETTE L88

$500,000 saw only 116 built in the model's final production year.

5 '53 CORVETTE

$300,000 if you can find one of the first 300 Corvettes ever made.

6 '63 CORVETTE Z06

$200,000 features a whopping 36 gallon gas tank.

7 '57 CORVETTE "FUELIE"

$130,000 for the first Corvette to feature fuel injection.

8 '55 CORVETTE

$113,000 for the first Corvette to offer a V8 engine, elevating the brand to high-performance level status.

9 '62 327/360 "FUELIE"

$100,000 has a 360 horsepower engine with fuel injection.

10 '96 GRAND SPORT CONVERTIBLE (LT4 engine)

$40,000 for a super-speedy Corvette that was only in production for one year.

MODS, RETROMODS, AND MORE

QUADRIPLEGIC RACER SAM SCHMIDT'S 2016 CORVETTE Z06

Professional Indy racer Sam Schmidt was on top of the world when everything came crashing down one fateful day. While practicing for the 2000 season, he crashed into a wall at 210 MPH. He was close to death and wasn't expected to leave a hospital bed for the rest of his life, but Sam pulled through. A quadriplegic, he is permanently in the driver's seat of a wheelchair, but he never gave up hope that one day he'd be behind the wheel of a race car again. Through determination, hard work, and help from a team of amazing engineers, seventeen years after his accident, Sam is back on the road and driving with a real driver's license. Sam is completely in control as he drives a very tricked-out 2016 Corvette Z06. The $1 million car is controlled by five infrared cameras that read Sam's eye movements to steer. He blows into a tube to hit the gas and sucks to brake, and is able to navigate a racetrack and public roads with relative ease, hitting top speeds of about 185 MPH.

RESTOMODS cost more than a restoration but sell for a lot less, since they're completely custom-built to the new owner's specifications. Want a green polka-dot interior? You can have it, but the cost will be high and the resale will be low enough for the new owner to undo the effects of your questionable taste preferences.

"For seventeen years, there has been very little in my life that I have 100 percent control over, but being in this car and driving is 100 percent under my control." — SAM SCHMIDT

THE MOST POWERFUL CORVETTE IN THE UNITED STATES?

THE CALLAWAY CORVETTE AEROWAGEN is a modification package that can be added on to an original Corvette Stingray. It takes the engine and supercharges it to 757 horsepower, taking the car from 0 to 60 in 2.7 seconds. It's been modded by Callaway, the same company that makes golf clubs. The price tag for the car plus the mod starts at about $130,000—a steep price but still less expensive than a Ferrari or a Lamborghini. One extra bonus of this mod: its "shooting brake" station wagon-sized trunk space is massive.

A SHOOTING BRAKE is an outdated term for a car that could hold a whole shooting party, including dogs, guns, and game. Now, the term is used in customized two-door luxury cars to describe a rear interior and trunk that has been converted into a station wagon trunk, suitable for carrying extra gear . . . like a full set of Callaway golf clubs, for example.

CUSTOMIZING A CLASSIC

Comedian and TV host Joe Rogan purchased a 1965 C2 silver Corvette Sting Ray convertible sight unseen, knowing that he would be customizing it with his own modifications. A big fan of the American muscle cars, Rogan wanted to amp up the performance and customize the look to make it uniquely his, with LS1, a hot suspension setup, and a new engine, along with custom solid wheels and a new interior. He showcased the final product on an episode of *Jay Leno's Garage*, which is available for viewing online.

ADD-ONS, OPTIONS, AND RPOS

RPO, OR REGULAR PRODUCTION OPTION, is a code created by General Motors that designates each car's specs when it leaves the factory during regular production. Designations include the base model first, then the options including paint color, engine, on-board information and entertainment, and wheels, along with any special equipment package codes, like Callaway.

MATCHING LUGGAGE

When you're not racing around the track or driving through town, you can still pledge allegiance to the car with Corvette-branded luggage, backpacks, totes, and other accessories, sold straight from the manufacturer or local dealer. Can't afford a Stingray? You can still pack in style with a five-piece Stingray luggage set. At just under $1K, you can get two rolling carry-ons, a backpack, messenger bag, and a duffel bag in black with the crossed-flags logo.

EVERYDAY DRIVING BECOMES A RACE CAR EXPERIENCE

The optional Performance Data Recorder records your driving experience through video capture, audio, and real-time performance data. After an epic driving experience, remove the SD card from the glove compartment and pop it into analytics software that can be downloaded from the Corvette website to get your driving stats. You can even replay your ride and experience it all over again from your home computer, tablet, or the 8-inch display on your dash while your car is idle. Valet mode keeps tabs on your baby while you're out on the town so you can enjoy yourself worry-free.

MAKE YOUR OWN ENGINE AND BE THERE AT THE BIRTH OF YOUR NEW CAR

Did you know that you can spend a day at the plant and help assemble the LT4 V8 engine that will ultimately go into your car? If you'd rather watch, you can attend the actual assembly of your car at the plant. And finally, once you attend your car's delivery at the Bowling Green plant, you can get a plaque on-site to commemorate the occasion. It can all be arranged through your local dealer or the National Corvette Museum in Kentucky.

The design was sleek and discreet, with a small, hood-mounted logo.

THE DESIGNER COLLECTION

CUSTOMIZING THE PERFORMANCE IS JUST ONE PART OF THE EQUATION. CORVETTE ALSO OFFERS INTERIOR COMFORT OPTIONS IN SUEDE AND LEATHER, ALONG WITH DESIGNER OPTIONS LIKE BLACK SUEDE, SPICE RED, TWILIGHT BLUE, OR A SPECIAL EDITION BRIGHT TENSION BLUE FOR THAT EXTRA LOOK OF LUXURY.

King of the Hill: ZR1
A match made in Stillwater, Oklahoma

The 1990 Corvette ZR1 could take a quarter-mile drag strip in 13.1 seconds at 110 MPH, earning it the name King of the Hill. The ZR1 can use any Borg-Warner six-speed manual transmission, but the real muscle came from the 375-horsepower, four-cam, 32-valve, all-aluminum, 5.7-liter V8 designed by Lotus and hand-built by Mercury Marine in their Stillwater plant.

The Indy 500 Edition

500 special edition pace car replica ragtops were made to celebrate the long-term relationship between Chevrolet and the Indy 500. 500 lucky owners got behind the wheel of a standard convertible with the Z51 performance package, loaded with high-end options like navigation and a Bose audio system. But the real reason to pick up this car was the eye-catching and instantly recognizable color scheme: Atomic Orange paint with gold ribbon stripes, adorned with Indy 500 badges for viewers who aren't already in-the-know. The rear view boasts a small spoiler, and from the side, admirers can ogle the silver split-spoke aluminum wheels.

Ron Fellows

Fans of racing know Ron Fellows as a champion in every major long-distance sports car race. Amateur racers know him as a charter member of Corvette Racing and the name behind the Ron Fellows Performance Driving School, the official high-performance driving school of the Corvette brand.

At the Spring Mountain Motor Resort and Country Club, just an hour's drive west of Las Vegas, car afficionados with a need for speed can take their driving to the next level with professional race car instruction, supervised and endorsed by the Canadian racer himself.

Still other fans know him as the name attached to the high performance Z06—the 2007 Chevrolet Corvette Z06 Ron Fellows Championship Edition. The Z06 comes in Arctic White with red accent stripes, one of which bears Fellows's autograph.

Only 399 Fellows Z06s were made in 2007 as part of this limited-edition run, 33 of which were shipped to Fellows's native Canada for initial sale.

1963 GRAND SPORT:
The Champion That Never Was

Zora Arkus-Duntov had plans to create a Corvette to rival the great American muscle car, the Shelby Cobra. He set out to build 125 ultra light Grand Sport editions to qualify as GT production cars. But when GM got word, they put a stop to it, citing a 1957 agreement not to provide assistance or participate in racing events. The run of just five cars resulted in an ultra lightweight car with a 550 horsepower engine. It would have been a great contender in its planned debut in 1963, but instead, GM replaced the small block 377 cubic inch motor with a heavier 427 and shipped the limited edition run of five cars off to private owners.

The five Grand Sports did race on notable tracks with legendary drivers at the helm, including Roger Penske, AJ Foyt, Jim Hall, Dick Thompson, John Cannon, Don Yenko, and Delmo Johnson. The original 1963 models are all restored and still exist today, valued at about $5,000,000 each.

SETTING THE PACE FOR THE INDY 500

The first time a Chevrolet was picked to lead the pack as a pace car for the Indy 500 was 1948, and 30 years later, 1978 marked the first time a Corvette earned the pace car honor. 2017 marked the fourteenth time a Corvette received that honorable position, more than any other car to date.

The 2017 pace car specs

The 101st race of the Indianapolis 500 was led by a Corvette Grand Sport with a Z07 package. It can go from 0–60 in 3.6 seconds, take the quarter-mile drag strip in 11.8 seconds—faster than the ZR1 King of the Hill.

Notable recent pace Corvette pace car drivers

Morgan Freeman, 2004
General Colin Powell, 2005
Patrick Dempsey, 2007
Guy Fieri, 2012

CORVETTE RACING TEAMS

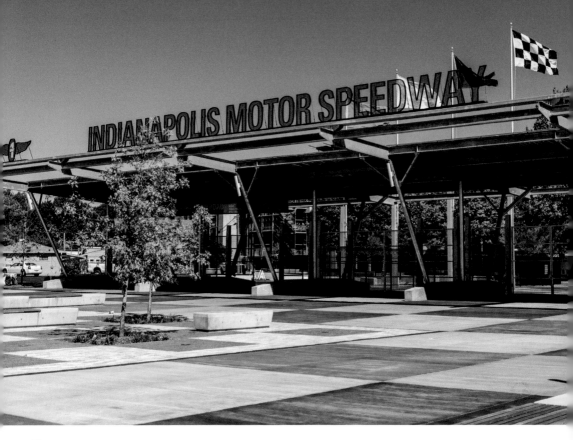

RICK MEARS

Rick Mears won the Indianapolis 500 in 1988 in Chevrolet's first-ever win. Mears drove a bright yellow, Penske Z-7 Chevrolet sponsored by Pennzoil. The car took the top spot for the next five years as well. That first year, in appreciation for driving Chevy to the company's first victory, Mears was awarded the first ZR1 Corvette ever made.

In 1990, Mears teamed up with Shinoda to design the Rick Mears Special Edition 1990 Corvette ZR1 with an aerodynamic body design that outperformed the regular production Corvette. Mears's involvement in the car was purely by accident. He had overheard a conversation between Shinoda and a colleague about plans for a new body kit, checked out the design, and wanted in. The rest was history.

FAST ✹ FACT

- **The team's first class win was in 2000, by Ron Fellows and Andy Pilgrim in a GTS.**

THE CORVETTE RACING TEAM

From its inception in 1999 to 2017, the Corvette Racing team has taken top prize in 105 races—more than any other professional racing team in North America—and was the first team to win 100 races. In 2015, the team took home the triple crown of endurance racing: the Rolex 24 at Daytona, Mobil 1 Twelve Hours of Sebring, and 24 Hours of Le Mans. The 2017 race car is the Corvette C7.R, the seventh generation racing vehicle. It shares a frame with the Z06, along with many of the top performance specs, making it the closest relationship between a high-performance race vehicle and a standard road car.

Celebrity Vettes

Fame by association: The list of celebs who favor Corvettes is long . . .
and some aficionados may surprise you . . .

George Clooney Voted *People* magazine's sexiest man alive in 1997 and 2006 favors the sleek, sexy styling of the '58 C1 V8 convertible.

Jay Leno An avid collector of cars, owns a few classic Corvettes, including a '63 Sting Ray, a ZO6 and the very first ZR1. Thanks to his video series *Jay Leno's Garage*, he was able to test drive a preproduction Z06, and realized how screaming fast the car is, taking the 659 horsepower engine down the canyon roads . . . only to be pulled over by a police officer.

Even those who have been knighted are driving Vettes, including **Sir Paul McCartney,** who can be seen in a C5, even though he has plenty to choose from in his homeland.

Mr. Tony Stark himself, **Robert Downey Jr.,** can be seen driving a '65 Sting Ray, which might even outdo the *Iron Man* character's collection.

Famous for just being famous is **Angelyne**, who had been a staple of Hollywood billboards throughout the 70s and 80s, always with her pink Corvette C4 by her side.

More notable celebrity Vettes:

Bruce Springsteen and his C2 Sting Ray convertible

Guy Fieri with an '07 C6

Will.I.am with a custom '59 C1

Slash's '66 Sting Ray coupe

Sly Stallone's custom '68 C3

Bruce Willis's '67 convertible

Gregg Allman's C6 convertible

ON THE BIG SCREEN

Cars and movies have always been a common combination, however the Corvette races to the top of the list. The range of movies the Corvette is in is unparalleled—not just in car-themed flicks, but in comedies, dramas, and just plain crazy, quirky movies. From movies all about the muscle car to tearjerkers like *Terms of Endearment*, America's most iconic car has starred in dozens of movies as a symbol of speed, success, sex, and adventure.

TERMS OF ENDEARMENT, 1983

This film won an Oscar for Best Picture in 1984, however some might say that the Corvette should've taken home its own prize at the awards if only for the abuse it took during filming. The poor car was driven along the beach and into the ocean.

CORVETTE SUMMER, 1978

The Corvette starred in a movie and had its name emboldened in the title—*Corvette Summer*, starring Mark Hamill. This movie was Mark Hamill's first post-*Star Wars* film project. The other star of the picture, a customized 1973 Corvette Stingray, was ultimately sold by MGM to a private collector in Australia.

Corvette Summer wasn't the only film to feature a Vette in the title . . . *Stingray*, (1978), was a typical late 70s madcap heist story about two drug dealers on the lam who stash their loot in a red Corvette Stingray parked in a used car lot. They return to find the car has been bought, and set out to chase down the new owners and recover their goods. Mistaken identities, chase scenes, and violence mix with comedy in this unusual and often forgotten ode to an unforgettable car.

In the 1971 cult film Billy Jack, *an enraged father berates his son for driving "a brand new $6,000" Corvette Stingray into the lake. In today's dollars, that's a $34,082 vehicle that went a-swimmin'.*

KISS ME DEADLY, 1955 One of the few films where the featured Corvette is a "new" car, A.I. "Buzz" Bezzerides's adaptation of Mickey Spillane's film noir mystery is set in Los Angeles. The 1954 Corvette looks especially gorgeous among the iconic landmarks and even the dark corners of the City of Angels, accompanied by dark poetry and even darker allusions to war and McCarthyism.

> "I'm a big car nut, so I put in all that stuff with the cars and the mechanic. I was an engineer and I gave the detective the first phone answering machine in that picture. I was having fun." —A. I. BEZZERIDES, *KISS ME DEADLY* SCREENWRITER

KING OF THE MOUNTAIN, 1981 No Corvette has been beaten up more on film than this thrashed 1967 coupe as it races up the winding, dangerous hills of Mulholland Drive. The car meets its fiery end just before the credits roll, in what some aficionados feel was a mercy killing for the car whose best days were well behind it.

> "Twenty-three miles of Mulholland, slicing Los Angeles like a knife . . . it's like a trip in time. Sometimes I just can't wait for night. You see too much in the sunshine. Road's changin' . . . civilization's choking it. At night, the straightaways are shorter . . . turns sharper . . . the drop steeper. It's the only place I ever felt safe. Clear, clean . . . and fast. Freedom. I wonder who it'll be tonight? I hope he's fast." —HARRY HAMLIN AS STEVE IN THE OPENING CREDITS OF *KING OF THE MOUNTAIN*

BOOGIE NIGHTS, 1997 This movie about porn star life in the 70s wouldn't have been complete without the ultimate sexy car-star of the decade, the "Competition Orange" 1977 C3. As Dirk Diggler's career declined, alas, so did his car.

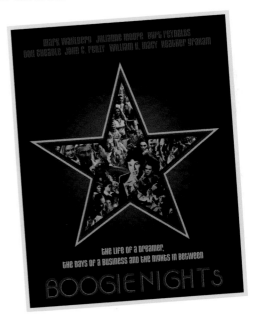

ANIMAL HOUSE, 1978 "Eric Stratton. Damn glad to meet you." The smooth president of the degenerate Delta House drives a gorgeous red 1959 Corvette C1. Unfortunately, his awesome car didn't stop him from getting completely pummeled by members of the rival fraternity, the Omegas.

Ivan Reitman produced *Animal House* and *Heavy Metal*, which both featured a cameo of an original Corvette convertible. Of course, the Vette in *Heavy Metal* was animated in Rotoscope while the real thing—in gorgeous mint condition—was actually present and driven on set and in the film.

THE SPY WHO SHAGGED ME, 1999

If you're an undercover secret agent looking to lay low, the last thing you want in a ride is a bit of flash. But Heather Graham's character, Felicity Shagwell, throws caution (and common sense) to the wind, driving around in a 1965 Corvette Roadster covered headlight to taillight in stars and stripes.

LIVE AND LET DIE, 1973

James Bond traveled to the U.S. for this voodoo-filled romp through New York City and New Orleans. When in America, Bond and his villains rode around in Cadillacs and Chevrolets as well as planes, buses, and taxicabs. But the villain, Mr. Big, had a car that stole the show. He drove a modified Vette, which was actually called a Corvorado—a mashup of a Corvette and a Cadillac Eldorado. The car, custom designed by Dunham Coach, wasn't put to rest when the film was in the can . . . it went on to be modified and used again in other films in different configurations.

BEWITCHED *BY CHEVROLETS*

Bewitched ran from 1964–1972 during the heyday of car sponsorships on broadcast television. Chevrolet was the main sponsor for much of the show's run, so classic car buffs love watching reruns with an eye toward what cars show up in each episode. While up-and-coming big city ad-man Darren Stephens always drove the latest Chevrolet models including Malibu, Corvair, and even a Camaro, his boss, Larry Tate, had the hottest car of them all: a bright yellow Corvette convertible.

GLEEKED OUT

GLEEKED OUT What type of car would you get if you wanted more excitement out of life? In season two of *Glee*, Mr. Shuester picked up a hot yellow Corvette convertible, although his rival for Miss Pillsbury's heart, Dr. Howell (played by John Stamos), definitely pulled off his red Corvette convertible better and more convincingly. It was all thanks to a Chevrolet sponsorship. The brand felt the small-town Ohio setting was a great vehicle for an iconic American brand from nearby Detroit. The team worked with *Glee*'s creators to integrate the brand within the show and in numerous publicity opportunities, but the double Vette appearance was the most memorable stunt of the campaign.

DALLAS *CAMEO* People may not remember Who Shot J.R. on *Dallas* (spoiler alert: it was his sister-in-law), but the cars that zipped around the ranch on *Dallas* were a memorable point for car enthusiasts. Season two, episode five featured an especially sexy black 1977 Corvette C3 with a T-top, sporting the license plate Ewing 5. It was a gift to Pamela Ewing (played by Victoria Principal) from her husband. The Vette was eventually replaced the following season by a black Porsche with the same plates.

THE FACEMAN'S WHITE 1984 CUSTOM CORVETTE

THE FACEMAN'S WHITE 1984 CUSTOM CORVETTE The *A-Team* features a gang of soldiers on the run who become guns for hire. This ordinary plot line was eclipsed by the high-powered action and chase scenes and hammy acting of the core four characters who made up the team. For work, they traveled in a nondescript black van, but Lieutenant Templeton Arthur Peck (AKA The Faceman or simply "Face") the group's resident con man in charge of commandeering vehicles and weaponry, drove a custom white 1984 Chevrolet Corvette with a red stripe and red interior. It was listed for sale on eBay in 2011 with a selling price of $40,000.

THE CORVETTES OF BEVERLY HILLS 90210

THE CORVETTES OF BEVERLY HILLS 90210 Brandon's Mustang, Dylan's Porsche, and Steve's Corvette vied for ultimate coolness. Steve Sanders's C4 sported the custom plate "I8A 4RE." Fast forward to 2015 and Steve was back in the Corvette driver's seat once again—this time in a black Stingray convertible.

ODES TO THE ICON

Popular icons like the Corvette take on meaning beyond their physical form. In song, a Corvette isn't just a car, it's a symbol of status, luxury, down-home Americana, sex, innocent fun, and even excess. The Corvette has made it into the lyrics of many popular songs. You can name the one by Prince, but how many more can you think of?

Tom Waits dove into chaos as he sang about tearing out the buckets of a red Corvette and other random acts of destruction in the 1983 song "16 Shells from a Thirty-Ought-Six."

Eiffel 65's song "Blue" is a testament to sadness, where everything the person in the song has and sees is blue. According to the lyrics, that includes his house, his girlfriend, and even his blue Corvette.

Brandy Clark wrote and sang a country song about the poor "Homecoming Queen" who didn't realize when she was seventeen that she wouldn't be the lovely young teen beauty for the rest of her life. Her dreams of sitting in her uncle's Corvette, waving to the crowd in the homecoming parade, are a distant sad memory. The song was remade by Sheryl Crow, who introduced it to pop listeners and widened its audience.

Country girl **Deana Carter** sang "I'm Just a Girl" about being a Chevy girl with an old Corvette, driving with the top down. Her model had a back seat for her friends, with a nod to Coca-Cola and the Beach Boys, too.

And country boy **Rhett Akins** tells the world he brakes for blondes in Corvettes in "I Brake for Brunettes".

"The One I Loved Back Then" by **George Jones** may be better known by fans as The Corvette Song.

Country music lovers don't have an exclusive when it comes to referencing the iconic automobile, however. Techno-pop acid-house singer **Praga Khan** sang of the luxurious jet-set life of a "Glamour Girl" in 2002. Of course the title character of the song drove a pink Corvette as she smoked her fancy cigarettes and lived life to excess.

THE STINGRAY ON THE B-SIDE

The Beach Boys loved to sing about cruising in cars almost as much as they liked singing about surfing and girls. Their song "Shut Down" is a tale about a race between about a 327 Vette and a 413 Ramcharger Dodge muscle car set to a typical upbeat Beach Boys surfer tune. Spoiler alert: the Corvette crushes it, of course.

"Superstock Dodge is windin' out and low

But my fuel injected Stingray's really startin' to go

To get the traction I'm ridin' the clutch

My pressure plate's burnin' that machine's too much."

LITTLE RED WHAT?

The car that inspired **Prince** to write his 1983 hit **"Little Red Corvette"** was actually a 1964 Mercury Montclair Marauder, which he helped bandmate Lisa Coleman buy at an auction in 1980. But "Little Red Marauder" wasn't quite as catchy as a song title.

The song "Little Red Corvette" was cited as the inspiration for the character Longfellow Deeds, played by Adam Sandler, in a loosely-based 2002 remake of *Mr. Deeds*, to buy everyone in his small town a brand new C5. The movie was filmed in the real-life small town of New Milford, Connecticut, and hired 350 locals as extras, along with thirty little red Corvettes.

THE **FUTURE** CORVETTE:
WHAT'S NEXT

The future looks so bright for the Corvette, we'll need to wear shades. The pending C8, ZR1 model in concept form is deemed to be "revolutionary." Rolling out in 2018, the model will be "powered by a version of the Corvette Z06's 6.2L LT4 V8 engine."

Will this mid-engine juggernaut have a model change? Rumors are abuzz in the automobile industry and only time will tell as to the future of GM's most famous sports vehicle. All we can say is that with some new patent-pending technology in the works, and talk about some big changes, the wait will be worth it.

The 2018 models will feature all of the iconic Corvette features with some exciting technological upgrades. 2018 will see the introduction of a new Corvette Carbon 65 Edition, which will be offered in the Grand Sport 3LT and Z06 3LZ models. This Carbon 65 Edition will showcase a carbon fiber exterior.

"The new Carbon 65 Edition honors that legacy, while offering customers another unique, special-edition model that personalizes the ownership experience."

—PAUL EDWARDS, U.S. VICE PRESIDENT, CHEVROLET MARKETING

The big reveal for the 2019 Corvette is planned for the 2018 auto show in Detroit with more advanced models rolling out.

All vehicles will have the modern enhancements such as HD Radio and high-resolution rearview camera displays. Of course there'll still be convertibles available for those looking to go topless … er, roofless!

FAST FACTS

Rumors circulating so far are:

- A hybrid model is in the works as GM recently trademarked the name "Corvette E-Ray"

- May include Zora in the name to pay homage to the legendary Zora Arkus-Duntov, the legendary "godfather" of the Corvette

- Included in lineup is the famed Stingray.

THE VIRTUAL DRIVING EXPERIENCE

VIRTUALLY A VIRTUAL VETTE

Grand Theft Auto included a virtual Vette that is virtually—but not quite—the same as the real thing. In the GTA series, they have a vehicle called the Coquette, which is modeled after the Corvette. The Coquette has changed over time as the series progressed, however it still mirrors the Corvette model changes, with the latest GTA (GTA V)'s Coquette resembling a C7.

Copying the Corvette to a T for a virtual racing experience are: Grand Turismo, Forza Motorsport, and Forza Horizon.

There are many other one off and series video games devoted to cars and racing that include Corvette into the mix. In fact, most fans agree that it wouldn't be a true racing title without providing gamers with an option to race with or in a Corvette.

CORVETTES IN VIDEO GAMES

Corvettes are an essential ingredient in video games, especially in this day and age, where you can play with lifelike graphics, almost creating an exact simulation of racing in a real Vette. Some games, like the Forza series, allow you to "purchase" rare Corvettes and sometimes even the ability to customize them.

Corvettes are so important in the racing and sports car genres of video games that they've even come out with a game specific to the General Motors model. The *CORVETTE* game was released in December 2003 for Xbox, and in March 2004 for PlayStation 2, allowing players to race with every Corvette ever made (from 1953 to 2003). Although the game came out to lukewarm reviews, it paved the way for future racing and car video game franchises to incorporate the iconic American vehicle, which would ultimately race against some of their fastest European competitors.

TOYS FOR SMALLER GARAGES

From electronic Stingrays to Barbie's famed
pink vehicle, Corvettes have been the car of choice
for kids and collectors for decades.

CRUISIN' WITH BARBIE

Barbie has been paired up with Corvette throughout the years as both American icons were born in the '50s. Barbie came out six years after the Corvette, in 1959, however she has been driving different versions of the vehicle, like a hot pink remote control Power Wheels convertible, from day one.

You can find these classic cars in mini form, designed for the most famous doll in history, on eBay and other e-commerce sites. They range from a vintage '60s classic to a hot '79 "super Vette" with remote control.

HOT WHEELS

Of course all the different Corvettes are represented in Hot Wheels form, with Stingrays, ZO6s, and more. The toy versions come at a much lower price tag and take up a lot less space, allowing you to collect all your favorite models without breaking the bank or renting out a small hangar.

SHOW YOUR VETTE SPIRIT

Devoted fans can find branded apparel available from dealers or directly from the company. But even the youngest fans can show their love of the brand with pride, carrying backpacks, lunchboxes, notebooks, pens, and more as well as wearing T-shirts that feature their favorite models.

PHOTO CREDITS